Original title:
Life and Whatever Else

Copyright © 2025 Creative Arts Management OÜ
All rights reserved.

Author: Finn Donovan
ISBN HARDBACK: 978-1-80566-225-9
ISBN PAPERBACK: 978-1-80566-520-5

A Journey by Candlelight

A flicker here, a shadow there,
We wander on with silly flair.
The wax drips down like melting dreams,
While laughter echoes, or so it seems.

With every step, a trip or two,
The floor is sticky, where's my shoe?
The glow is weak, but spirits high,
We dance beneath the stubby sky.

Starlit Paths and Footprints

Under stars so bright and wide,
We tripped and tumbled, what a ride!
A path of glitter, oh so sleek,
We mapped our way with giggles unique.

Each footprint tells a funny tale,
Of slipping frogs and slippery snail.
A cosmic laugh, a wink, a grin,
Now where's my shoe? Oh, let the fun begin!

Musings on the Edge of Tomorrow

Tomorrow's here, or so they say,
But I forgot what's on today.
With coffee spilled and socks askew,
I ponder deeply, what to do?

A thought floats by, it's quite absurd,
I'll chase it down, oh wait, a bird!
Through time I leap, with utmost grace,
And land right back in yesterday's place.

A Palette of Emotions

With colors bright, I start to paint,
A canvas full of giggles, quaint.
Blues for blues, and greens for glee,
A splash of red, just wait and see.

Oh look, a smudge, it's quite a mess,
But who am I to second guess?
With every stroke, my heart takes flight,
Creating joy in shades of light.

A Tapestry of Small Wonders

In the morning, the toast burns,
But the cat starts to purr,
A dance in the butter,
On the edge of a stir.

The socks in the dryer,
Are playing hide and seek,
While the toast yells, 'I'm crispy!'
The coffee's feeling sleek.

The plant thinks it's a tree,
But it's only a sprout,
With dreams of the ocean,
And a life full of doubt.

The clock ticks away loudly,
A comedic refrain,
While we chase our own tails,
In this curious game.

Flickers of the Human Spirit

There's a man with two left feet,
Who dances like a bird,
With socks on his warm hands,
And a wig made from fur.

A cat wearing a hat,
Struts across the floor,
While a dog drags a snack,
And lies down for more.

The fish in the bowl,
Has secrets to share,
But bubbles just float,
No one ever cares.

With laughter and giggles,
We bounce off the walls,
In this zany adventure,
Where the silliness calls.

Finding Harmony in Dissonance

A penguin with shades,
Slides down the steep hill,
While a parrot recites,
An old vampire's thrill.

The clock sings a tune,
That goes "doodly doo!"
While slippers start dancing,
On their own, who knew?

The microwave beeps,
With timing so wild,
As our dinner burns bright,
Like a misbehaved child.

In the chaos we find,
A sweet kind of grace,
Like juggling rubber ducks,
In a baffling race.

Portrait of a Day Gone By

The morn arrived, a bit late,
Socks mismatched, oh what a fate.
Coffee spills on my best shirt,
Guess today I'll don that dirt.

Lunchtime laughs, the bread went stale,
The sandwich swapped a dog's big tail.
In meetings, my thoughts took flight,
Daydreams led me into night.

Evening snacks, the fridge is bare,
Hoping there's still pie somewhere.
Tomorrow's list? Just one more snooze,
Who needs plans when you can cruise?

Mosaic of Colors

Red is for the apples tossed,
Yellow's lost, the lemon's frosted.
Blue's for jeans that make me cheer,
Green's for envy when none is near.

Painting walls in shades of fun,
Jokes drawn out, by everyone.
Life is bright, like highlighter marks,
Let's paint the town with silly sparks.

Doodles thrive amidst the mess,
In chaos, find your happiness.
A splash of joy, a stroke of glee,
This canvas of absurdity.

The Fluidity of Being

Woke up feeling like a star,
Then tripped on my dog, oh how bizarre.
Breakfast danced in my cereal bowl,
Milk spilled out, oh what a soul!

Tried to jog, but walked instead,
Turns out I like my comfy bed.
Sweatpants whisper, 'Stay awhile',
Embrace the couch with a silly smile.

During dinner, I wore a bib,
Food on face, I lose my fib.
Wine poured out, perhaps too much,
Laughter flows, a joyful clutch.

Echoes Across the Years

Childhood times, with games we played,
Jumping ropes and ice cream made.
Memories linger, like a song,
How did I get here, and what went wrong?

Teenage fads, with hair so big,
Dancing on tables, doing a jig.
Now I laugh at all those styles,
Photos from then bring out the miles.

Grown-up mishaps, like a trend,
Forgot my keys, wait, was that a friend?
Hip replacements? Well, maybe not,
Life's a comedy, give it a shot.

Whispers of the Unseen

In shadows where the secrets play,
A spatula sings the blues all day.
It turns the pancakes with a twist,
A chef's delight that can't be missed.

The cat's convinced it runs the show,
As it declares, 'I'm in the know!'
But really, what's the hidden scheme?
A world of mischief and a dream.

The toaster chats with the tea pot,
About the crumbs that they forgot.
They giggle in their kitchen car,
Stirring chaos, not so far.

So raise your cup to things unseen,
To thumping hearts and laughter keen.
In every nook where whispers blend,
We find the joy that has no end.

Between the Pages of Time

A time traveler trips on his shoe,
Where's he going? Not a clue!
He flips the pages, what a mess,
So many chapters, can't confess.

The socks get lost, but not alone,
They form a club to take the throne.
With mismatched stripes and patterns bold,
Together they weave a tale untold.

A sandwich once vowed to be a hero,
To save the world from bland, oh dear-o.
But mustard's laughter takes the lead,
In this saga of bread and seed.

So dance around those timeless pages,
With silly fables of all ages.
For every flub and silly rhyme,
Is just a step in sacred time.

Echoes of Forgotten Dreams

Beneath the bed, there lies a beast,
It feasts on socks, a cozy feast.
With every nibble, echoes sigh,
'Where have all my slippers gone?' 'Oh my!'

The world is bright with circus clowns,
That juggle life in polka crowns.
While bubbles float like dreams of yore,
They pop with giggles, asking for more.

An umbrella dreams to touch the sky,
While puddles hold their breath nearby.
In each reflection, laughs abound,
A carnival where joy is found.

Let's toast to dreams that dance away,
In laughter's grip, they choose to play.
For every echo that we hear,
Is a reminder: fun is here!

The Dance of Fleeting Moments

A waltz with socks upon the floor,
They twirl and spin, then ask for more.
As dust bunnies cheer them on with pride,
What a silly, wild ride!

The clock ticks loud, a playful jest,
It's in a hurry, but we know best.
We laugh at every tick and tock,
And play hopscotch with each ticked block.

A sandwich sandwiching a fable,
Wants to be the sweetest label.
With jelly smiles and peanut cheer,
It dreams of a picnic, oh so near.

So join the dance of fleeting time,
With silly steps and rhythm rhyme.
For every moment, quick and sweet,
Is just a jig, a silly feat.

The Weight of a Single Breath

A balloon floats high with glee,
Yet pops in laughter, just like me.
I hold my breath, it's quite a feat,
Just to find out—air tastes sweet.

Like socks that vanish in the wash,
Or cats that plot to gain the posh.
I gasp and chuckle, lose my way,
Breathin' in giggles, day by day.

A sneeze that turns to rocket flight,
Is just my way of taking flight.
So take a breath, and hold it tight,
For every giggle brings delight.

In tiny moments, joy will sprout,
Like popcorn popping, hear the shout.
The weight of breath can lift a gloom,
And telling jokes will seal that room.

Curiosities in a Whirlwind

In a world where spoons can dance,
And chairs suggest a bold romance.
I'm swept away by socks and hats,
As they engage in playful chats.

The sun is winking, clouds do tease,
While ice cream trucks play hide and seize.
A butterfly wears a tutu bright,
While pondering the meaning of flight.

With ketchup bunnies and mustard fish,
A dandelion's absurd wish.
Imagine the chaos of a cake,
That dreams it's a pie, oh for goodness' sake!

As I twirl in this wild mayhem,
The echoes of giggles seize my hem.
In every swirl, a chance to grin,
In whims and wonders, let's begin.

The Rhythm of Laughter and Sighs

A clown slipped on a banana peel,
And now, my friend, that's how I feel.
With chuckles mixing in the air,
We dance around our silly flair.

The raindrops sing a jazzy tune,
While umbrellas play the sax at noon.
A sigh escapes, but laughter thrives,
The comical rhythm—oh how it jives!

A cat in pajamas on a tree,
Claims to be the best, can't you see?
As the world spins with comic flair,
We wade through chuckles without a care.

In every sigh, a punchline hides,
Like clowns that ride on wild tides.
Together, we juggle much delight,
In laughter's rhythm, all feels right.

Threads of Connection

With yarn and jokes, we weave and spin,
Connecting the dots with a cheeky grin.
A patchwork quilt of goofy dreams,
As we navigate absurdist themes.

My shoe's untied, but oh so fine,
It leads the dance, a goofy line.
In tangled threads, our stories blend,
As laughter echoes, we transcend.

With paper planes and misfit socks,
We launch our thoughts, like airborne blocks.
In every twist and quirky turn,
New friendships spark, as we all learn.

So hold my hand, let's stitch the night,
With giggles bright, it feels just right.
For every bond, though strange it seems,
Is sewn in laughter, shared in dreams.

Navigating Through the Fog

In the morning mist, I trip on a shoe,
Hoping the road leads to something that's new.
My GPS insists, 'You're right on the path!'
But I can't see a thing, just a cat doing math.

Waving at strangers, they stare and they frown,
As I bumble through streets of my own silly town.
The birds sing in chorus, as if it's a jest,
But I swear they're mocking my quirky bequest.

The Art of Letting Go

I tried to hold onto my unmarked balloon,
But it slipped through my fingers, now gone to the moon.
I watch it float up, like my dreams in July,
Each wave of release makes me giggle and sigh.

The weight of my worries, I toss in a stream,
As ducks quack in chorus, they join in my dream.
The chaotic release feels like dancing in rain,
What once was a burden now tickles the brain.

Serenade for the Ebb and Flow

The sea pulls me in, then it just lets me go,
Like a friend with a joke, but I'm not in the know.
I splash and I tumble, like a fish out of place,
Waves giggle and whisper, 'You've got style and grace!'

As I dance with the tide, my feet twirl so free,
Ocean's a comedian, it's all about me.
With each push and pull, we've made quite a show,
An ebb and a flow, what a wonderful glow!

Reflections in a Puddle

Jumping in puddles with glee on my face,
I spot my reflection in the splashy embrace.
A puddle of nonsense, my thoughts swim about,
Waving at raindrops when I'm feeling down and out.

Each ripple a giggle, each drop a small cheer,
The world's a big laugh when the weather's not clear.
So let's dance in the rain, make a splash and a mess,
In puddles, we find joy, who needs all the rest?

Echoes of Forgotten Dreams

In a world where socks disappear,
I chase the thoughts that spark my cheer.
Like cookies crumbling on the floor,
I ponder what I dreamt before.

The cat sings opera on the chair,
While I debate if I should care.
With cereal in a coffee cup,
I realize I am just a pup.

The clock ticks loud, yet time stands still,
A dance of whims, a silly thrill.
Balloons float high, like hopes once strung,
Yet here I am, just being young.

So raise a toast with fizzy drink,
And laugh aloud while you still think.
For echoes of those dreams gone by,
Are just as real as we can fly.

Between Laughter and Tears

A sneeze erupts, I spill my tea,
My shoe's untied, oh woe is me!
I trip on air, the world's a joke,
Yet laughter's here, I guess I'm woke.

Chasing shadows in the street,
With pies on windows that call for defeat.
I smile at cats who twist and turn,
For every laugh, we live and learn.

Between giggles, the wisdom flows,
Like mustard on a stuffy nose.
We wade through puns and silly fears,
In this strange dance of truth and cheers.

So come and trip, and laugh with me,
Let's spill the beans, just wait and see.
For in this mix of smiles and sighs,
Is where we find our sweet surprise.

The Currency of Breath

Each breath I take is worth a dime,
I spend it all on jokes and rhyme.
With wheezing laughs and wheeling glee,
I barter for my cup of tea.

In queue for life, we stand and sway,
Trading dreams for yesterday.
With hiccups loud and whispers sweet,
I save my cash for silly treats.

Each giggle costs a penny spent,
On memories that might prevent
Regrets from piling like dirty socks,
While I count blessings, counting clocks.

So let's invest in every breath,
For laughter's riches conquer death.
In this mad scheme, we chase the worth,
Our treasures found right on this earth.

Imprints on the Path of Being

Footprints left in muddy grass,
With slip-ups made that make me laugh.
I trip on dreams, they wink and say,
Come join the dance, don't fade away.

A hotdog flies, a bird on quest,
As happy hearts prepare for zest.
With every giggle, steps unfold,
Like stories shared, like tales retold.

Between the stumbles and the grins,
Are all the chances where joy begins.
We stumble forth, with hope in tow,
Leaving traces in the ebb and flow.

So let us march, hand in hand tight,
Through silly storms, we find the light.
For every step, a laugh we glean,
In this wild ride, we reign supreme.

Gardens of Unraveled Chaos

In gardens where the daisies twirl,
The gnomes get dizzy in a whirl.
We plant the seeds of our grand schemes,
Yet end up sipping lemonade with dreams.

Mismatched socks upon the grass,
A butterfly takes flight, oh what a class!
We chase our tails, and laugh in glee,
While weeds grow taller than the trees.

The cat holds court, a furry king,
While squirrels debate the fruits of spring.
Amidst the laughs, a snail darts past,
Yet here in chaos, fun is cast.

So raise a toast to our dear mess,
With spilled ideas that we confess.
In gardens wild, we twirl and play,
Embracing chaos day by day.

Raindrops on the Windowpane

Raindrops dance like little sprites,
As we watch roads turn into sights.
Each puddle splashes laughter, too,
Reflecting dreams of me and you.

The cat meows a soggy tune,
While clouds parade beneath the moon.
We count each drop, a silly game,
And wonder if they have a name.

Old umbrellas turn inside out,
A fashion statement, without doubt.
We slip and slide on pavement slick,
As thunder claps, oh what a trick!

So let's embrace this watery show,
With rubber boots, to splash and go.
In nature's mix, we'll find our way,
As raindrops laugh and dance today.

Silhouettes of Tomorrow's Echo

In shadows cast by setting suns,
We dream of races yet to run.
The future whispers with a grin,
While we guess the shape of what's within.

A juggler's caught in time's quick game,
As echoes chant a silly name.
We paint our hopes in hues of cheer,
While socks and shoes disappear!

The clock ticks on, a comic show,
With antics only we would know.
Laughter fills the bustling air,
As tomorrow's echoes lose their care.

So let us jump from shadowed glee,
Embracing every mystery.
With silhouettes, we carve our place,
In quirky moments, faces lace.

Navigating the Sea of Days

In a boat of mismatched chairs we row,
Across the waves of to and fro.
The starfish wave, the seagulls squawk,
As jellyfish do a jig on the dock.

We chart our maps with crayons bright,
Sailing past clouds, what a sight!
With snacks in hand, we sing the blues,
While dolphins laugh at our silly views.

A compass spins, oh what a fuss,
We guess our course, it's all a plus.
With laughter loud, we ride the swell,
In a kiddie pool, we cast a spell!

So here's to sailing through the haze,
With crew of friends, we'll find our ways.
In the sea of days, we freely drift,
Embracing the chaos, what a gift!

The Soundtrack of a Thousand Moments

In the cafe, a cat played jazz,
A barista spilled a cup of pizzazz.
With each sip and laugh, we danced like fools,
Our worries lost in frothy bubbles and drools.

The busker strummed the strings of the street,
While pigeons strutted to the offbeat.
A kid tripped on a skateboard with flair,
And everyone cheered, forgetting the air.

Old folks bickered over who won the game,
While seagulls stole fries, adding to the fame.
The sun set low, painting the sky,
A masterpiece where moments fly high.

In every giggle, every clink of glass,
Life's silly moments come and then pass.
We're just the actors in this grand play,
With unexpected joy leading the way.

Canvas of Changing Seasons

Spring arrived with a sneeze and a shout,
Flowers bloomed like kids breaking out.
Summer brought sunburns and ice cream drips,
While bees did the tango on wildflower hips.

Autumn shrugged in a cloak of brown,
Pumpkin spice chaos spread through the town.
Leaves made a ruckus as they danced from trees,
While squirrels hoarded snacks like they were on a spree.

Winter tiptoed in with a frosty wink,
Snowflakes falling, and kids made a stink.
Hot cocoa spilled on a sweater's design,
And snowmen stood proudly, sipping on wine.

Each season, a canvas of laughter and cheer,
With mishaps and giggles that we hold dear.
At every turn, a new tale unfurls,
Painting our days with the brightness of swirls.

Chasing the Infinite

Racing down roads in a quirky old car,
We laughed at the GPS, our guiding star.
With snacks piled high and music so loud,
We chased sunsets, feeling ever so proud.

A signpost pointed to nowhere at all,
We stopped for a picnic, heedless of the call.
A squirrel joined us, eyeing our bread,
While a crow swooped in, full of mischief and dread.

Each bump on the road was a tale to tell,
With twists and turns where chaos befell.
We roamed like dreamers, carefree and free,
Chasing the infinite, just you and me.

So here's to our journey, wherever it leads,
In laughter and moments, we plant all our seeds.
Life's a wild ride, full of charms and spins,
In this wacky adventure, true joy begins.

Fragments of a Wish

A penny tossed in a fountain of dreams,
Echoes of laughter burst at the seams.
Wishing for fortune and maybe a dog,
But all I got back was a foggy smog.

I wished for romance on a carousel,
Instead, I found a ride that made me unwell.
With every spin, my heart did a flip,
While popcorn kernels danced on my lip.

Hopes thrown like confetti in the breeze,
Some stuck to my hair, even in trees.
A wish for tomorrow, but what about today?
If things get silly, who cares what they say?

So here's to the wishes—some land, some don't,
In the quirks of the journey, we always won't.
Embrace every fragment, the strange and the fun,
For in the odd moments, our hearts have truly won.

Celebrations of the Small

In a seed, there's a tree,
But it mostly just waits to be.
A tiny bug gives a cheer,
While a snail takes a selfie, I fear.

A crumb on the floor is a feast,
For ants, it's a party, at least.
A shoe left behind stirs delight,
As it struggles to dance through the night.

A hiccup makes laughter arise,
And a sneeze brings twinkling eyes.
Confetti of dust in the air,
Means your socks must have flair!

So let's toast with our juice cups high,
To the moments that flutter and fly.
For the smallest of things bring the best,
Like a cat in a box, seeking rest.

Whispers of Past Lives

Last week my pants were a hit,
This week they no longer fit.
A fortune cookie once said,
There's a mouse in your bread.

My neighbor swears he was a cat,
Spending days on a soft, warm mat.
But now he bakes scones so fine,
While trying to walk a straight line.

A goldfish claims he was a knight,
In bowls fought to keep his crown bright.
With a flick of his tail he confesses,
His battles were all with lettuce stresses.

Whispers of old speak in jest,
Of mischievous tales that could jest.
In a world of tales, big and small,
Not a one will win the brawl!

The Comfort of Familiar Strangers

In a cafe, we pretend to know,
The barista, who steals the show.
With a wink and a smile, he brews,
Mysterious drinks with quirky views.

The mailman waves with a grin,
Like he's just uncovered a win.
Yet, is he from the planet of mail,
Or just a guy, with a great detail?

The lady with cats by her side,
Has more secrets than any guide.
With her stories, she fills the air,
Like a comic book without a care.

With strangers, there's comfort to find,
In a world that can often be blind.
A nod, a laugh, or a strange glance,
Turns the ordinary into a dance!

Colors of a Transient Day

Morning wakes in a fuzzy haze,
With toast that's too burnt to praise.
The sun yawns with bright, silly rays,
As birds chirp out their rehearsal plays.

Noon arrives dressed in vibrant hues,
With clouds playing peek-a-boo views.
The grass wears a coat of fresh dew,
While squirrels plot their afternoon crew.

As twilight paints a canvas in gold,
The laughter of friends with stories retold.
While shadows stretch like legs so bold,
Whispering secrets too silly to hold.

Night wraps its arms with stars in tow,
Whispering dreams that ebb and glow.
In colors of moments, our hearts lay,
A spectacle found in each fleeting day.

Shadows of What Could Be

In the corner, shadows dance,
A cat in a hat, taking a chance.
Dreams flutter like moths in flight,
Chasing the fridge light, oh what a sight.

Maybe I'll be a famous chef,
Whipping up snacks, nothing too deft.
Or a squirrel in a tree with style,
Claiming my acorns with a silly smile.

Thoughts rattle like cans in a bin,
In the race of my mind, I just can't win.
Hurdles of laundry, dishes in piles,
Yet here I am, laughing for miles.

Tomorrow I'll soar, or trip on a shoe,
The shadows giggle, they know what I'll do.
In the moon's glow, plans often flee,
But who needs a map? Let's just be free!

Tapestry of Random Encounters

The bus stop's a stage for oddity's show,
A bee in a bow tie, a llama in tow.
With all of the quirks that strangers possess,
Each little moment's an unplanned success.

One chap in a tutu, sings off-key tunes,
A lady with bread rolls, she's feeding the moons.
They argue with pigeons, it's quite the display,
Who knew on this corner, it'd be such a play?

A lost cup of coffee, a split on the floor,
Reminds us that chaos can open a door.
To laughter and joy hidden deep in the day,
Where misfits unite in the silliest way.

So here's to those moments, the woven delight,
Of strangers and laughter that feel just so right.
In a world full of quirks, let's dance to the beat,
Embrace every chance, even that man with bare feet!

A Symphony of Little Things

In the kitchen, a pop and a fizz,
A spatula dances like it's in a quiz.
The toaster cheeps out a crispy tune,
While jellybeans plot in a cheeky swoon.

Naps on the couch, so blissfully brief,
With dreams of adventures, stolen by belief.
The clock ticks slowly, a playful tease,
As cats refine their art of expert tease.

Mismatched socks on the floor, parade,
An orchestra of chaos, the finest charade.
With laughter as notes, they play on repeat,
Highlighting the joy in even defeat.

In the garden, daisies hum a sweet song,
And shadows play tag, oh, what could go wrong?
With whimsies and giggles tucked under each wing,
Life's a grand symphony, making us sing!

Beneath the Surface of the Ordinary

Underneath the surface, a turtle's got flair,
Wearing shades with style, like it doesn't care.
It sips on some seaweed, checks its phone,
Joining the party in its ocean throne.

The mailman's got gossip that's hard to believe,
As he juggles the packages, ready to leave.
Cats whisper among themselves, eyes aglow,
Planning a coup against the vacuum, you know?

The garden hose gurgles, it's plotting a trip,
To a land of green grass where flowers can skip.
And the old garden gnome with his mismatched hat,
Dreams of adventures, oh what's more than that?

Beneath every rock, there's a riddle to find,
Whims in the world, a quirky design.
So let's join the laughter, it's all on the way,
In the ordinary stories, let's dance and sway!

Ripples in a Still Pond

A frog jumped in with quite a splash,
He surely thought he made a dash.
But as he sat in muddy glee,
The fish just chuckled silently.

The sun reflected in a swirl,
A dragonfly began to twirl.
With every ripple, laughter grew,
As turtles joined, and so they blew.

The lily pads began to dance,
They swayed along, oh what a chance!
Through all this splash and funny play,
The pond sighed softly, 'What a day!'

In stillness, chaos found its way,
Yet here we find, we're all okay.
For in the ripples, joy expands,
A little laughter never lands.

The Language of a Whisper

Two cats conspire on the fence,
They plot mischief, oh so dense.
With eyes that gleam, they share a scheme,
To knock down that old canister dream.

A breeze comes by, it's not too shy,
It joins in gossip, oh my, oh my!
The flowers giggle, their petals twitch,
While rabbits snicker, they find the niche.

The world knows secrets wrapped in air,
Like squirrels plotting without a care.
The trees extend their branches wide,
As if to say, "Come, let's confide!"

In whispers soft like morning fog,
They laugh about that old lost dog.
For in this chatter, one can see,
The joy of secrets, wild and free.

Driftwood Dreams on the Shore

A piece of wood from days of yore,
Waves lap gently, it dreams of more.
With messages from sailors bold,
It chuckles softly at tales retold.

Seagulls squawk with glee and flair,
As boats drift by without a care.
The sand says, "Come, let's have some fun,"
While sunbeams dance, oh, what a run!

Each grain of sand, a little jest,
As tides tease with an endless quest.
The wood just smiles, a timeless sage,
Wishing for a laugh on every page.

In driftwood dreams, where time is shy,
It dances with stars in the evening sky.
For on this shore, where stories gleam,
Lies the humor in every dream.

Fleeting Seasons in a Jar

Autumn leaves in a jar of glass,
A squirrel peeks in, oh, what a pass!
With acorns stacked like tiny towers,
He chuckles at the waning powers.

Winter's breath, a frosty treat,
The jar is cozy, oh, what a feat!
Snowflakes giggle as they settle down,
While penguins dance in their little town.

Spring comes in with a burst of cheer,
Tiny buds whisper, "Summer's near!"
They sway and sway, a funny show,
With bees that fly and flowers that glow.

In seasons wrapped, we find our glee,
In every jar, a memory.
So let's hold tight to moments dear,
And laugh along, year after year.

Gentle Reminders of Wonder.

In a world where socks go flee,
Are they lost, or just playing free?
Far from feet, they roam the floor,
Always hiding, who knows where they soar?

Coffee spills, a morning cheer,
A splash of joy for all to hear.
Cereal dances, what a sight!
Breakfast chaos, pure delight!

Chasing dreams on a lazy day,
With thoughts that wander far away.
Lemonade in hand, we grin,
Who knew that mess could feel like win?

Crumbs of laughter on the way,
In the silliness, we choose to stay.
Embrace the antics, let them flow,
In the midst of chaos, love may grow.

Ebb and Flow of Existence

Life's a wave, ride it high,
With silly fears that drift on by.
Pick up seashells, toss them back,
In the current, we make our track.

Raindrops tap on a window pane,
Counting puddles just seems insane.
Dancing under clouds of gray,
Who knew that storms could be this sway?

Whimsical thoughts in the breeze,
Chasing butterflies with such ease.
A dance of chance in all we do,
With every mishap, we start anew.

Laughter echoes, fills the night,
Unscripted joys, oh what a sight!
In this ebb and flow we find,
That searching prompts us all to bind.

Whispers of Untold Journeys

Little creatures on the move,
In their world, they find their groove.
Ants parade like tiny kings,
While crickets play their funny strings.

Clouds above, all shapes and sizes,
One looks like food, oh what surprises!
Tasting dreams with candy stars,
In a universe that's truly ours.

Grass stains on my favorite jeans,
From tumbles and those silly schemes.
Rolling down a hill with glee,
Is adulthood just grown-up play, you see?

Chasing after hiccups with flair,
Who knew giggles float in the air?
In each journey, a secret beckons,
Funny tales where joy connects and reckons.

Fragments of a Fleeting Moment

A glance in time, a fleeting grin,
Catching minutes as they spin.
Who knew a wink could hold such weight?
Silly moments create our fate.

Jellybeans and ice cream dreams,
The world is bursting at the seams.
With every slip and little shout,
We find our way, that's what it's about.

Chairs that squeak and floors that creak,
Echo the tales that feel unique.
With splendid messes and spills of cheer,
These fragments remind us, joy is near.

From whispers soft to laughter grand,
Moments trickle like grains of sand.
In this mosaic, we paint our way,
With colors bright to greet the day.

The Serenity of Ephemeral Moments

A butterfly flits by, oh so brief,
It lands on my nose, causing me grief.
We share a laugh, then it flutters away,
Reminding me joy can be here and sway.

A cup of coffee spills, oh what a sight,
The dog leaps up, thinks it's a delight.
We slip and we slide, it's all such a game,
In chaos we thrive, yet nothing's the same.

A shoelace unties at the worst possible time,
As I trip and I tumble, I'm in my prime.
I laugh on the ground, and I'm not alone,
The world keeps on spinning, while I make my throne.

Moments are fleeting, yet full of cheer,
Like socks in the dryer, they disappear.
Cherish the madness, the giggles, the fun,
For when we look back, we'll see we've just run.

Kaleidoscope of Choices

I woke up this morning, my socks mismatched,
Decided to embrace, not to get attached.
Pizza for breakfast? Why not give it a spin?
In this circus of choices, it's funky to win.

Should I wear a hat, or let hair flow wild?
My neighbor's cat stares, as if I'm a child.
Should I dance with the mailman, or wave him goodbye?
In this world of confusion, I choose to comply.

A salad or chips? What a silly debate!
Each bite of bad choice makes my lunch just first-rate.
The trick is just laughing, when choices collide,
In this kaleidoscope world, you've got to abide.

One day I'll be wise, or so they all claim,
But right now I'm just riding this funny old game.
So spin me around like a top on the floor,
And I'll always find joy when choosing for sure.

The Pulse of the Unfamiliar

New flavors surprise me, I'm taken aback,
A pickle on pizza? Now that's quite the snack!
I shudder and smile, and dive in the deep,
What's weird becomes tasty, in this chuckling heap.

A dance with a llama? Sure, why not?
It winks as it twirls, then ties me in knots.
I laugh with delight, such a quirky affair,
In the pulse of the strange, I find love in the air.

A ticket to nowhere? I'm booking the flight,
Just me and my shadow, we'll party all night.
In bizarre company, I'm crazily free,
The pulse of the wildly unknown calls to me.

So I'll dance with the oddities, no time to fret,
For normal is boring, and I've no regret.
Embrace the absurd, let the heart lead the way,
In the saga of weirdness, it's a funny ballet.

Capturing Time in a Bottle

A jar full of giggles, a splash of the sun,
I ponder the chance of capturing fun.
Each bubble a memory, a burst of delight,
As I bottle the moments that twinkle at night.

A sneeze in a meeting? Oh, what a scene!
The boss's face shifts, caught in between.
I snicker and chuckle, as the clock ticks away,
This jar holds my laughter, come what may.

A dance with old photos, swirling around,
Each flicker of memory, a joy that I've found.
Footloose in the past, with no stress or guile,
I capture the echoes, and bottle each smile.

So here's to the jar, may it never grow stale,
With flavors of moments, of laughter, of tales.
Here's to the nonsense, the quirks that we share,
In this treasure of times, we're always aware.

Canvas of Infinite Possibilities

The paintbrush dances, colors collide,
Splatters of joy on a whimsy ride.
Each stroke a giggle, each hue a grin,
A masterpiece born from chaos within.

From scribbles of thought to rainbows in air,
Surprises await in the bold and the rare.
With palettes of laughter, we're all artists here,
Creating our tales without any fear.

So grab your bristles, let's mix and let's play,
The canvas is vast; we can color the day.
With dots and with dashes, the story takes flight,
In a world full of wonder, every wrong is a right.

Let's splash in the puddles, or paint the sky blue,
In this wild studio, there's always room for you.
With each new creation, our giggles will grow,
On this canvas of chaos, let humor overflow.

The Alchemy of Moments

Mix a dash of laughter, add a pinch of fun,
Stirring up mischief 'til the day is done.
In potions of giggles, we find our delight,
Transforming the mundane into pure, silly flight.

Brew time for the magic, let the chaos commence,
In this whimsical lab, nonsense makes sense.
Experiments bubbling with joy and with cheer,
We concoct our own happiness, year after year.

The potion's not perfect, sometimes it will spill,
But who needs precision when the thrill's such a thrill?
With quirky elixirs and sprinkles of glee,
We toast to our moments, come mix up with me!

So gather your friends, let's whip up a blast,
In this wild alchemy, let's make memories last.
For each laugh is a treasure, a secret we share,
In the cauldron of smiles, let's stir without care.

Unfolding the Mystery of Now

What's hidden in seconds, what's tucked in a smile?
The magic unfolds with a wink and a wile.
Each tick of the clock is a riddle to heed,
In the great game of moments, don't forget to proceed.

A sneeze or a snort could spark a delight,
The ordinary becomes a whimsical sight.
In waiting for buses or chatting in lines,
We discover the joy in these curious signs.

Let's tiptoe on sunshine, dance through the breeze,
Finding treasure in trials, a lift with each tease.
For mysteries deepen with each heartfelt cheer,
In the now that's unfolding, let laughter be near.

So let's savor these moments, both silly and sweet,
In the puzzle of living, each piece is a treat.
With giggles like confetti, let's cherish and vow,
To uncover the magic that's happening now.

Sunlight Filtering Through the Trees

Beneath the canopy, giggles abound,
As sunlight plays tag with the shadows around.
The leaves start to shimmer, a bright, laughing hue,
In this leafy ballroom, let's boogie for two.

The branches are chandeliers of sparkles and glee,
While squirrels hold their meetings, plotting with glee.
Nature's a jokester, with puns in the breeze,
As we tumble and roll on the ground 'neath the trees.

A chorus of rustles, the wind sings a tune,
As we sway like the branches, dancing with the moon.
With a skip and a hop, let's frolic and flee,
In the forest of laughter, forever carefree.

So come take a stroll through this bright, leafy maze,
With sunlight filtering in, let's bask in the blaze.
For amidst all the whispers and rustling with ease,
The world's a big joke, and we're the best tease!

Portraits of a Wandering Heart

With mismatched socks on parade,
I wander streets that never fade.
Each corner holds a hidden joke,
In every laugh, a story's cloak.

A bird once asked where I was off,
I shrugged and said, 'To find some scoff.'
The trees just laughed, they know my scheme,
To chase away the mundane dream.

Clouds giggle with their cotton sheen,
They whisper secrets, soft and green.
I skip through puddles, dance and twirl,
A wandering heart, a playful whirl.

Through bustling towns and sleepy lanes,
I gather smiles like precious gains.
With every step, my shadows grow,
Painted in hues that never show.

The Mosaic of Everyday Wonders

The morning toast burns bright and bold,
Yet butter spreads as stories unfold.
A teapot whistles a quirky tune,
Filling the air with spicy festoon.

Sock puppets hold a daily meeting,
Debating crumbs, their foes, retreating.
The cat convinced she rules the house,
Catches her breath, then chases a mouse.

Neighbors wave from porches near,
As I dodge a frisbee, overcome by cheer.
The mailbox groans with junky mail,
Yet every flyer tells a tale.

At dusk, I toast to chocolate cake,
In this mosaic, a laugh we make.
Each day a patch in wacky thread,
Stitched with giggles, never with dread.

Ramblings of a Curious Mind

Why do ducks walk in straight lines?
As if they're plotting secret signs.
A squirrel told me a riddle profound,
But I forgot it, spinning around.

At the café, spoons in a whirl,
Stirring gossip, a swirling twirl.
The sugar bowls conspire with glee,
Making me dance, oh my, oh me!

A chipmunk's stash: peanuts galore,
Seems like he's holding out for more.
What does he know that I can't see?
A secret life beneath the tree.

Amid these ramblings, I might confess,
Curiosity leads to delightful mess.
With a wink, the world comes alive,
In this puzzling dance, I thrive.

Chasing Fireflies in the Twilight

As darkness falls, fireflies ignite,
Little lanterns in the night.
With a jar and dreams, I scamper fast,
In this twinkling chase, my worries pass.

Giggles echo, the breeze takes flight,
Dancing shadows, oh what delight!
I trip on roots with clumsy grace,
Yet every stumble's a joyful embrace.

The stars above join in the fun,
Winking down, one by one.
I catch a glow, it flickers bright,
A tiny spark in the vast twilight.

Each moment's fleeting, like those lights,
A treasure found in joyful sights.
I'll chase them all, until the dawn,
These fireflies' glow, forever drawn.

Beneath the Surface of Routine

Each morning brings a brand new fight,
Coffee spills and socks in flight.
The cat's a ninja, quick and sly,
While toast erupts, oh my, oh my!

The clock ticks loud, a laughable beast,
I rush for breakfast, not a feast.
Traffic jams like snails on parade,
Yet in this chaos, dreams are made.

The neighbor's dog joins in the chase,
Chasing squirrels with endless grace.
Weird joy found in daily strife,
Spin the wheel, it's such is life!

So here we are, all quirks and glee,
In this topsy-turvy jamboree.
Routine can dance like a silly song,
When you roll with punches, you can't go wrong!

Shadows Dancing in the Dusk

As daylight fades, the shadows play,
Twisting shapes in a cabaret.
A tree becomes a giant's arm,
The streetlamp winks, oh what a charm!

A squirrel struts like a tiny king,
With acorn treasures, his bling-bling.
While crickets start their evening tune,
The stars peek out, a cheeky boon.

Laughter echoes from nearby homes,
As evening whispers in funny tones.
The moonlight spills a silver smile,
And time slows down for just a while.

So gather 'round, the night's a treat,
With dancing shadows, life's upbeat.
Embrace the dusk with arms wide out,
In this merry world, let's twist and shout!

Threads Woven in Time's Fabric

Bright threads of morning, dark threads of night,
We stitch our journey with laughter and fright.
Each faux pas, a loop of the loom,
Creating a tapestry in every room.

A spot of coffee, a dash of cheer,
Old socks hiding, oh dear, oh dear!
The cat claims the best seat in the house,
As I trip over shoes that should be quite doused.

Mismatched socks tell their own tale,
Of laundry days gone quite stale.
Yet every fabric, ragged or neat,
Holds memories that make us complete.

So let's weave together, both old and new,
In colorful patterns, a vibrant view.
Each moment a piece, in this grand design,
Embrace the chaos, everything's fine!

The Color of Unwritten Chapters

With pages blank, oh what a tease,
A pen in hand, let's write with ease.
Adventures waiting in lines to fill,
I scribble dreams with quirky thrill.

A dance of pencils, colors collide,
As clumsy rhymes take us for a ride.
Each errant stroke, a laugh, a cheer,
In moments missed, we find our sphere.

Ink spills stories, both silly and grand,
Of trips to nowhere and a pet band.
So scribble nonsense, let go of fear,
With each wild thought, the world feels near.

As chapters unfold, let's jump and twirl,
In this book of jest, let joy unfurl.
With every laugh, and every blunder,
We splash color in life's sweet wonder!

Flickering Lights in the Distance

In the twilight glow, they dance and sway,
Hoping to find their own bright way.
But they trip on wires and laugh out loud,
While the shadows giggle, hiding in a crowd.

Bouncing around with a cheerful fright,
They flicker and fumble, what a sight!
"Are we stars or bulbs?" they pondered well,
As a squirrel scratched his head, unable to tell.

Each blink a secret, each flick a tease,
They chase after dreams like a bee to the bees.
"Look at us shine!" one yelled with glee,
Little do they know, it's just the TV.

So onward they flicker, chasing their fate,
With beams of confusion, they don't hesitate.
For in their spark, we find pure delight,
In the curious dance of the endless night.

The Flavor of Solitude

Banana peels slip, and the cat's on a spree,
Ten paws of mischief—where could they be?
In our kitchen of quiet, the teapot sings,
While the toaster plots what tomorrow brings.

A cup of calm brewed, with a side of fun,
The salad is anxious, but the bread's well done.
Dancing with shadows on the wall,
Who knew being alone could feel like a ball?

We share our secrets with walls so tall,
"Do you think we'll ever have a guest-call?"
A spoon answered back, quite filled with sass,
"Why bother? We're fabulous, just let it pass!"

So let's toast to silence, with a pinch of cheer,
Our quirky galas held, with not a soul near.
As laughter erupts from the avocado spread,
In the flavor of solitude, we feast ahead.

A Chronicle of Unraveled Paths

Once upon a time, roads twisted and turned,
Each one a riddle, each lesson learned.
Duck crossed the street without a care,
Whipped cream on pancakes, a sweet affair.

One path led to shoes that squeaked at dawn,
While another made socks disappear, so gone!
A rabbit in boots hopped with great pride,
Finding lost buttons from a canary's ride.

The compass spun wild, like a confused bee,
Navigating fields of fruity ice tea.
Each fork in the road a giggling mess,
Where paths intertwine, what a fun excess!

With laughter as fuel and joy as the map,
The journeys continue, no time for a nap.
In this chronicles of chaos, we take our stand,
Embracing each turn, with a wink and a hand.

Sunbeams on a Rainy Day

Clouds are grumpy, holding back cheer,
But here comes a sunbeam, bright and clear!
With rain boots dancing in puddles below,
Who knew splashes could steal the show?

A breeze with a giggle tickles the trees,
While pinwheel wishes sail in the breeze.
Umbrellas spin like hats on the fly,
As rainbows arm wrestle the clouds in the sky.

"Let's skip that nonsense, and splurge on fun!"
Shouted a sunbeam, "Come join me and run!"
With laughter echoing from each droplet's kiss,
Turning gray moments to splashes of bliss.

So we twirl through the chaos, heart full of play,
In sunbeams emerging on a rainy day.
A comedy act in the sky's big parade,
Where every mishap gets joyfully played.

Riddles of an Open Sky

Up high, the birds play chess,
With clouds as their fancy board.
The sun, a referee with a smile,
As shadows jump and explore.

Each fluffed-up cloud spills a joke,
While moonbeams whisper sweet lies.
The stars giggle at our odd quests,
As ants march under vast skies.

They plot with crumbs from packed lunches,
Imitating our human feats.
Oh, the mischief in their tiny heads,
Dreaming big with little feet.

So let your spirit soar and twirl,
In riddles from above bestowed.
For in this goofy, endless dance,
We're merely guests on the road.

Reflections in a Coffee Cup

Stirring thoughts in dark brew,
Swirls of cream laugh at the rush.
Frothy dreams float on the edge,
While spoon touches the rim with a hush.

Coffee beans discuss their past,
Trading tales of morning strife.
One claims he rode a bus to work,
The other insisted he saved a life.

But steam lifts secrets to the sky,
Whispers tickle sleepy minds.
In every yawn, a story brews,
Of casual siestas that mankind finds.

So let's sip and giggle away,
Each gulp is a jest, a surprise.
With every drop, reality fades,
And imagination sweeps us high.

Chasing the Fragile Dawn

Moonlight tiptoes in ballet shoes,
As the sun pleads for a chance to shine.
They dance the twist of time and space,
Trading tunes like perfectly matched wine.

A sleepy cat watches the show,
Eyes half-closed, dreaming of mice.
While crickets take their last bow,
Rehearsing for their final slice.

The flowers yawn, stretching high,
Each petal whispers to the sun.
'We'll share this stage, don't be shy,'
As light begins, day has begun.

So chase the dawn, with all your might,
For fragile moments slip away.
In laughter shared, we chase the light,
And kick start another day.

The Weight of Unspoken Words

In silence, secrets stack like bricks,
Building castles unwittingly high.
Each glance a message, heavy and thick,
Like a pie crust left out to dry.

Words waltz around, too shy to speak,
Their faces hidden, playing coy.
While thoughts bubble up to their peak,
Searching for that golden joy.

An awkward smile begins the fight,
Can you hear the laughter trapped inside?
Muffled giggles in twilight's light,
As courage takes on its wild ride.

So let's unleash the playful jest,
Toss those bricks, let spirits fly.
For in the weight of words suppressed,
We find freedom—oh me, oh my!

Mosaic of the Unseen

In a world where socks go missing,
The other halves hold a secret glistening,
A mismatched dance, a style so brave,
Creating fashion from the laundry cave.

Underneath the couch, crumbs keep their throne,
They whisper stories of meals once sown,
These tiny treasures in soft shadows hide,
While poodles prance in a feline stride.

Llamas may leap without a care,
But it's the goldfish that always stare,
Watching us humans, so grand and wise,
While they judge our snacks with bulging eyes.

Bubbles float in the morning air,
Each one a dream of a dentist's chair,
They pop with laughter, a winking jest,
Life's a circus, so wear the best!

Seasons of the Soul

Winter's chill brings frosty noses,
While sneezing fits keep us in poses,
Snuggled in blankets, we binge and snack,
Who knew hot cocoa could steal a whack?

Spring arrives with a sneeze and a clap,
Suddenly flowers steal the map,
Pollen attacks with a tickle, a tease,
Allergies rule, bringing us to our knees.

Summer days with ice cream drips,
We chase the sun while our sunburns grip,
Laughter echoes from every corner,
As we dance in swimsuits, oh what a foreigner!

Autumn brings cider, sweet and hot,
Pumpkins abound in a dance with rot,
Crunching leaves make a savory sound,
Nature's slow dance as we twirl around.

Navigating the Unpredictable

Monday mornings, we seek caffeine,
Like sailors lost in a routine,
Our maps unclear, but we sail on ahead,
Chasing dreams made of banana bread.

Tuesday's twist throws us a curve,
A flat tire makes us lose our nerve,
With duct tape in hand, we make our stand,
Becoming Einstein, our own handyman.

Wednesday comes with a surprise sprint,
A coffee spill, oh the world's glint,
Dancing on tables, we embrace the laugh,
As chaos reigns, we copy the giraffe.

Thursday struts with a thunderous clap,
Where shoelaces tangle, like a candy trap,
But we jump around with the heart of a kid,
In the circus of life, we hardly hid!

Flickers of Joy in the Mundane

On Tuesday nights, the trash can hums,
As old pizza boxes dance to drums,
Garbage day brings a raucous cheer,
We salute the moon while we hold our beer.

The cat bounces off a wall with style,
Confused by its own feline guile,
While mailboxes spy on the secret round,
Letters giggle with gossip sound.

Dishes pile high like a mountain's peak,
Each plate a trophy that we do seek,
In this epic battle of soap and foam,
We laugh out loud, feeling right at home.

And when shadows dance in the fading light,
We toast to the silly, the absurd, the slight,
For in every wrinkle of our long, winding tale,
There's joy unfurling, beyond the pale.

Embracing the Chaos

In the morning rush, I spill my tea,
Cats leap high, as if to flee.
Juggling socks, I miss my shoe,
This perfect morning, askew but true.

The toaster pops, a toast to fate,
I'm late again, oh isn't it great?
With mismatched socks, I prance outside,
Embracing the chaos, I take it in stride.

Dancing in traffic, what a sight,
Drivers stare, some may take flight.
Silly moments, wrapped in grins,
In this wild world, everyone wins.

So raise your cup, let's cheer, my friend,
For each mess means the fun won't end.
In twisted paths, we'll surely find,
That chaos here is by design.

Spheres of Influence

Round and round the universe spins,
Who knew that chaos could bring such grins?
My tiny circle got even smaller,
But with my cat, I'm the king and baller.

Friends texting memes, who needs the news?
They say to change, but I refuse.
In this bubble, we laugh and play,
Orbiting joy, come what may.

The bookshelf's shaking, what's that about?
Probably just my dance moves, no doubt.
Gravity jokes while we make a plan,
To conquer snacks, and be a fan!

With pizza slices as our currency,
We govern with laughter, oh can't you see?
In spheres of fun, let's keep it light,
Influencing joy, every day and night.

Unraveled Thoughts at Dusk

As sunsets paint the sky with flair,
My brain unravels with the evening air.
The dinner burns, oh what a smell;
A masterpiece? I guess you can't tell.

With thoughts astray like wayward kites,
I ponder deeply, through curious nights.
A sock is missing, where could it be?
Maybe it's off having fun with me!

Fleeting ideas flutter and dart,
Funny how they slip, then depart.
I laugh at shadows, dancing on walls,
In this twilight, nonsense enthralls.

So gather your dreams and give them a whirl,
For dusk brings magic, give it a twirl.
Unraveled thoughts, the best kind of mess,
At day's end, we embrace silliness.

The Weight of Unspoken Words

In the silence, I hear a laugh,
What's heavy here, a math problem's half?
Silly thoughts swirling like autumn leaves,
With each word, a giggle that weaves.

I wanted to say how I feel at lunch,
But all I managed was a half-hearted munch.
Jokes die in silence, like old pizza crust,
So I write them down—oh, that's a must!

With every missed chance, my heart does ache,
Yet laughter bubbles up, for humor's sake.
The weight of whispers that never were,
Plays in my head, this internal blurr.

So let's toast to guts, and risks we take,
To blurt out jokes, for heaven's sake!
Guest speakers of quips, we'll never fade,
With unspoken words, let's make our parade!

Serenade of the Everyday

Woke up late, forgot my socks,
Tripped on shoes, dodged the clocks.
My breakfast turned into a race,
A dance with toast, what a disgrace!

Coffee spills like morning dew,
Mug half-full, but I'm brand new.
The world spins on its silly axis,
Chasing dreams that twist and tax us.

To do lists grow like garden weeds,
I plant a thought, but it recedes.
Life's a joke, and here's the catch,
I'm just the punchline in the batch!

So let us laugh, for joy's a must,
A comedic twist in every thrust.
With quirky steps, we waltz through days,
And paint our paths in silly ways.

Mosaic of Hopes and Regrets

A sock in hand, the search begins,
My favorite one, but where's its twin?
Lost in the couch, or maybe the car,
A quest for fabric, excellent bizarre!

Chasing dreams like bubblegum,
They pop so quick, can't find the sum.
Regrets tiptoe, a silent parade,
While hopes jump high in a wild charade.

I book a trip to climb a hill,
But trip on thoughts that give me chills.
A map of wishes, drawn with flair,
Yet some lead nowhere – that's just unfair!

In the mosaic of silly vibes,
I stitch my hopes with goofy jibes.
Together we laugh, through thick and thin,
In the tapestry we wear with a grin.

The Stillness Between Heartbeats

In the quiet, what do I hear?
The sound of snacks disappearing near.
A surprise attack on a bag of chips,
My heartbeat syncs with crunching quips.

Minutes stretch like silly putty,
Time plays tricks, a bit too nutty.
Heartbeats pause for a puppet show,
A dance of seconds, twirl and glow.

Thoughts collide in the quiet space,
Chasing driftwood, a rabbit's race.
I find a joke in each small pause,
What's the punchline? Here's a clause!

With laughter echoing through the gaps,
I juggle moments — no time for naps!
In stillness, I brew a silly stew,
With every heartbeat, I cook up new.

Beneath the Stars of Ordinary Nights

Stars twinkle like a disco ball,
While crickets chirp, they start to call.
An evening stroll with flip-flop flairs,
Beneath the moon, we dance with glares.

The night is young, with pizza dreams,
And laughter flows like bursting seams.
Each shadow plays a role so bright,
In the glow of overwhelming light.

Fireflies buzz with socks of glee,
They light the way, like sparks of tea.
A cosmic giggle in a twinkling show,
Ordinary nights, put on a glow!

So here's to whimsies, silly sights,
To clumsy steps and starry flights.
We revel beneath the silly skies,
In moments where the fun never dies.

Threads of Memory

In a world where socks go stray,
I ponder on that fateful day.
When all my thoughts took off and fled,
Leaving just crumbs and a bowl of bread.

A cat on the roof sings a tune,
While I search for my missing shoe.
Is it a ghost, or just my brain?
Sometimes I think I'm going insane.

Old photographs stacked high in a pile,
Of friends who haven't seen me in a while.
Each snapshot a story, each grin a delight,
Like a fashion show gone very wrong one night.

Fleeting moments weave through my mind,
Like a half-cooked pasta left behind.
I laugh at the mess that time has made,
And raise a toast to the dreams that played.

The Canvas of Now

With paint splatters bright and bold,
I start a chapter I once told.
But the story took a turn and I lost my way,
Now I'm doodling suns on a rainy day.

Where are the brushes? I can't find one!
Maybe the cat has stolen my fun.
While pondering life over a cup of glue,
I decide macaroni art might just do.

My canvas shakes and the colors collide,
As I trip on a paint can, what a ride!
Creativity's clutter, a glorious mess,
But isn't chaos sometimes the best?

With laughter and flourishes, I create my fate,
In a world where weird is wonderfully great.
Here's to the masterpiece yet to be shown,
An abstract of moments that we've all known.

Chasing Shadows

I spotted a shadow that looked just like me,
With a silly grin and a glee full of glee.
We danced through the park, we made quite the scene,
Until it flipped over and turned into a bean.

Now who am I chasing? That pesky reflection,
In a puddle, a window—what a connection!
It winks and it grins in the sun's warm glow,
And hides when I'm near, playing hard to show.

My past and my future do a waltz in the breeze,
While I trip over shadows and laugh with some ease.
I bought a new hat, hoping it'll stay,
But it leaped off my head and ran away!

So here I am, chasing a ghost in the light,
With laughter a-bubbling, oh, what a sight!
A whimsical romp through the streets of exist,
Fleeting moments I'll miss, but joy's hard to resist.

Reflections in a Broken Mirror

In shards of glass that twist and gleam,
I see a jester, caught mid-scream.
His shoes too big, a hat too tall,
He's laughing at me as I trip and fall.

Fragments of moments, a scene so absurd,
Like a flock of chickens who've all lost their word.
Each crack a story, each line a jest,
Maybe the chaos means I'm blessed?

The man in the mirror is quite a sight,
He dances like nobody in the moonlight.
With mismatched socks and a cheeky grin,
He dares me to laugh, to let the fun begin!

So here's to reflections, both silly and bright,
In this wacky world that feels just right.
For even in shards, there's beauty around,
In the mess of it all, laughter might be found.

www.ingramcontent.com/pod-product-compliance
Lightning Source LLC
Chambersburg PA
CBHW051630160426
43209CB00004B/590